MELODY BOBER

All Creatures Great...
But Small

Notes from the Publisher

Composers In Focus is a series of original piano collections celebrating the creative artistry of contemporary composers. It is through the work of these composers that the piano teaching repertoire is enlarged and enhanced.

It is my hope that students, teachers, and all others who experience this music will be enriched and inspired.

Frank J Hackinson

Frank J. Hackinson, Publisher

Notes from the Composer

Did you know that . . . .
. . . a woodpecker's tap may be his form of email?
. . . fish have a great sense of smell?
. . . the loon is the Minnesota state bird?

These fun facts accompany my newest elementary collection
"All Creatures Great . . . But Small"–pieces designed to give young beginners a sense of musical styles through a variety of critters!

Students will experience the two-step with Teddy Turtle and staccato sounds in "The Woodpecker Song." They will learn E♭ in "Stanley, the Skunk", and enjoy the expressive moods of "Sparrow Song" and "Lucy, the Lovely Loon." Crossovers, dynamics, and octave changes make each piece exciting, challenging, and fun to learn.

The selections have optional teacher duets which I encourage you to use, as they enhance the style and mood of the pieces and give your student a boost of confidence at recital time.

I hope students and teachers alike will enjoy this collection as they learn about music and about the many creatures great . . . but small.

Melody Bober

Melody Bober

Contents

Teddy Turtle's Two-Step

Turtles are the oldest form of reptile alive today, with very little change in their 200 million-year history.
They are the only reptiles with a shell built into their skeletons.

Melody Bober

Lively (♩ = ca. 152)

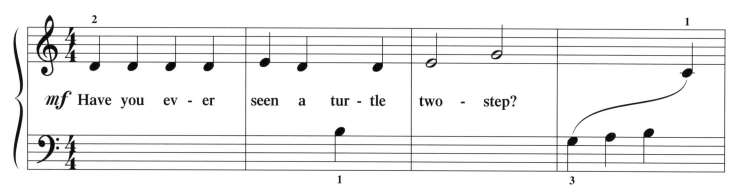

mf Have you ev - er seen a tur - tle two - step?

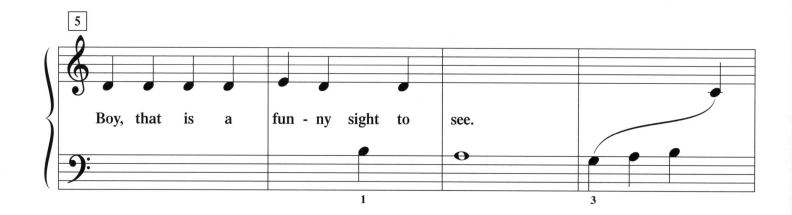

Boy, that is a fun - ny sight to see.

Teacher Duet: (Student plays 1 octave higher)

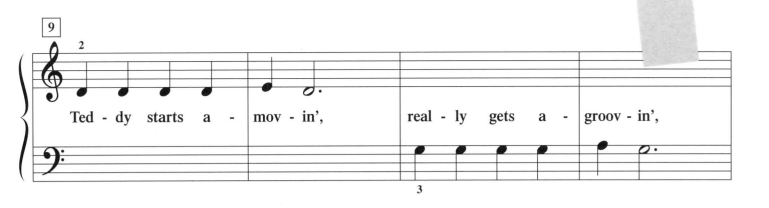

Ted - dy starts a - mov - in', real - ly gets a - groov - in',

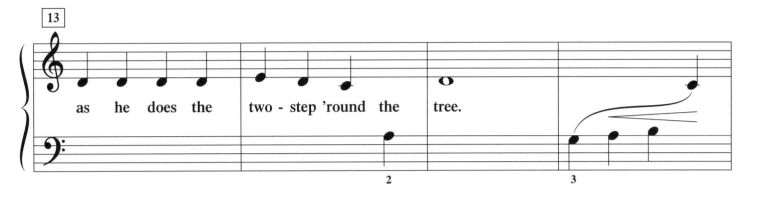

as he does the two - step 'round the tree.

f Ted - dy does the two - step just for me!

6

The Woodpecker Song

The woodpecker's very straight and hard pointed beak is used to search for insects;
but it is also used to hammer, drum, or tap, in order to communicate.

Brightly (♩ = 80-96)

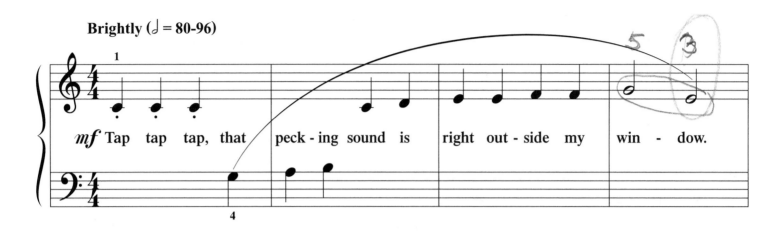

mf Tap tap tap, that | peck-ing sound is | right out-side my | win - dow.

Tap tap tap, | rap rap rap, | there he goes a - gain. Oh!

Teacher Duet: (Student plays 1 octave higher)

mp

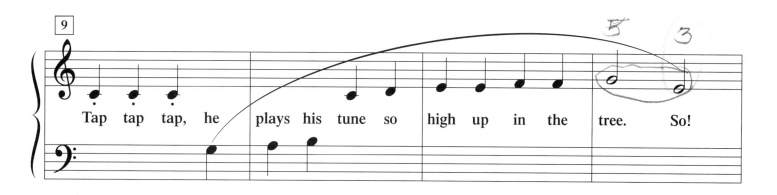

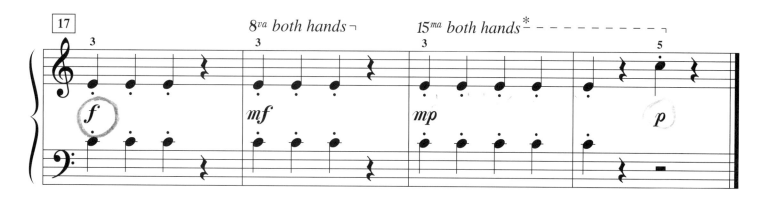

* Jump up 2 octaves.

FJH1640

Prickly Pete, the Porcupine

Porcupines are vegetarians. Their babies are called "porcupettes."
Thousands of quills on their backs provide plenty of protection.

Seriously (♩ = ca. 116)

Both hands 1 octave lower throughout

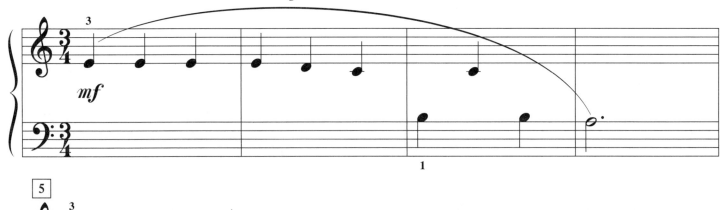

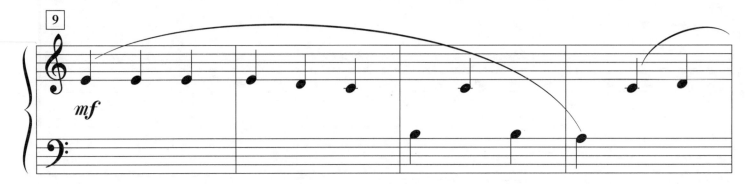

Teacher Duet: (Student plays 1 octave lower)

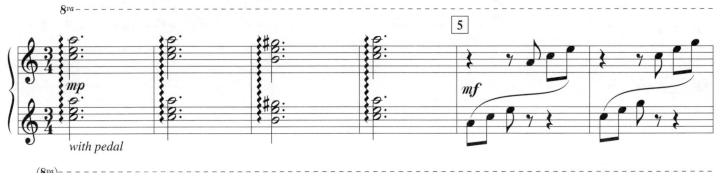

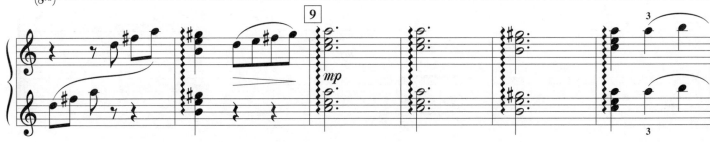

Stanley, the Skunk

Skunks are members of the weasel family.
They move slowly and have strong front feet and long nails that are perfect for digging.

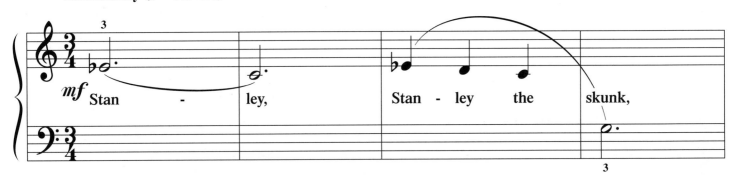

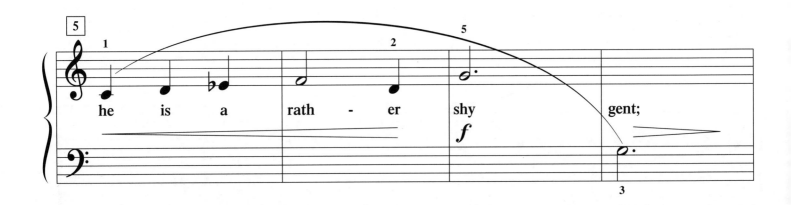

Teacher Duet: (Student plays 1 octave higher)

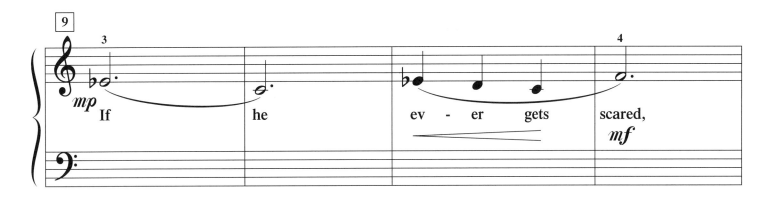

If he ev - er gets scared,

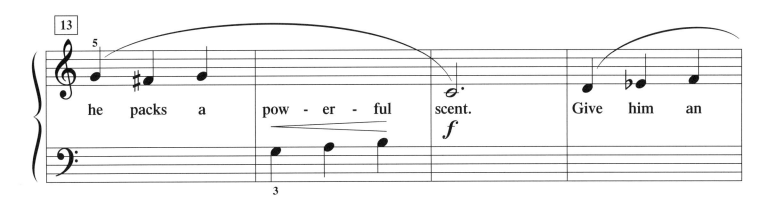

he packs a pow - er - ful scent. Give him an

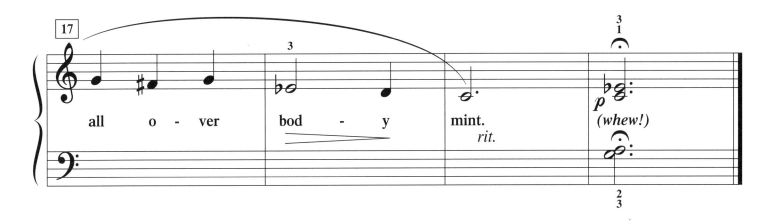

all o - ver bod - y mint. (whew!)

Ricky Raccoon

Raccoons are "omnivores" – they will eat just about anything!

Sneakily (♩ = 152-160)

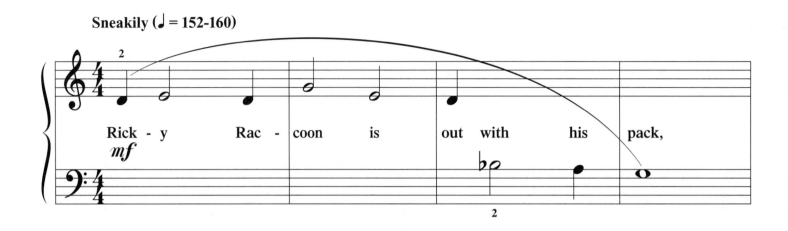

Rick - y   Rac - coon   is   out with   his   pack,

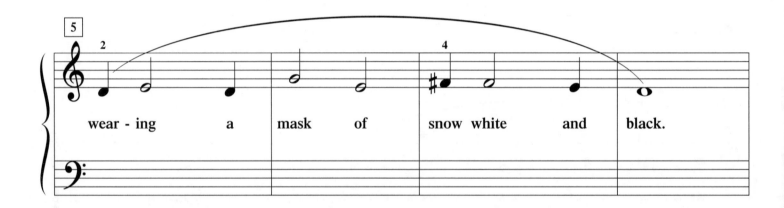

wear - ing   a   mask of   snow white   and   black.

Teacher Duet: (Student plays 1 octave higher)

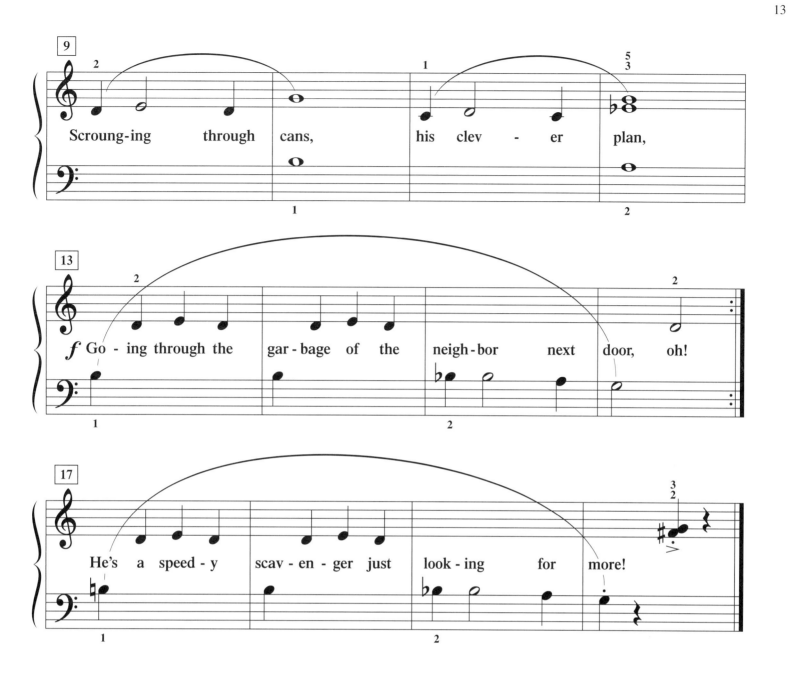

Scroung-ing   through   cans,   his   clev - er   plan,

f Go - ing through the   gar-bage   of   the   neigh-bor   next   door,   oh!

He's   a   speed - y   scav - en - ger   just   look - ing   for   more!

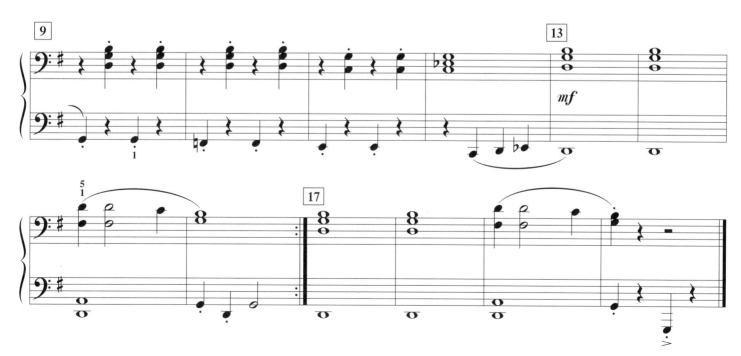

mf

FJH1640

The Sparrow's Song

When temperatures are cold, song sparrows must eat up to 4,000 seeds per hour
to maintain energy levels.

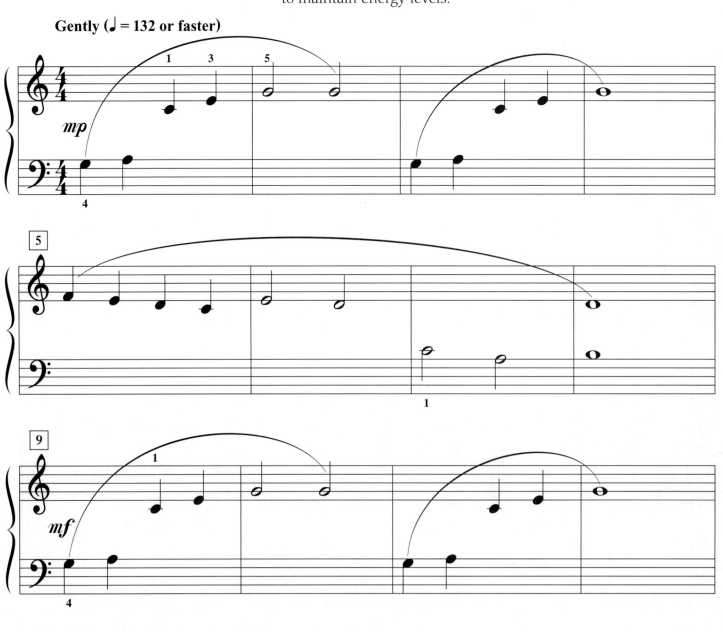

Teacher Duet: (Student plays 1 octave higher without pedal)

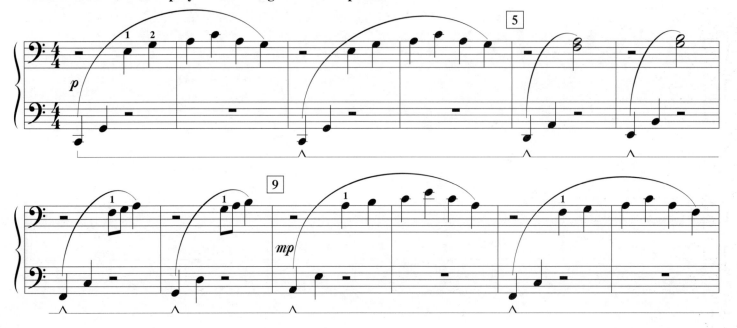

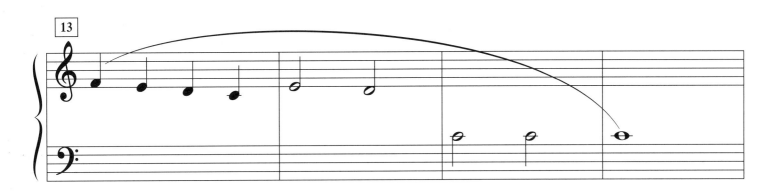

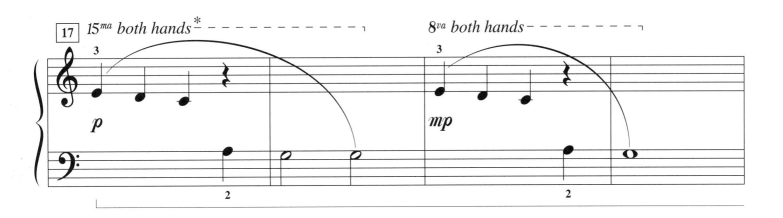

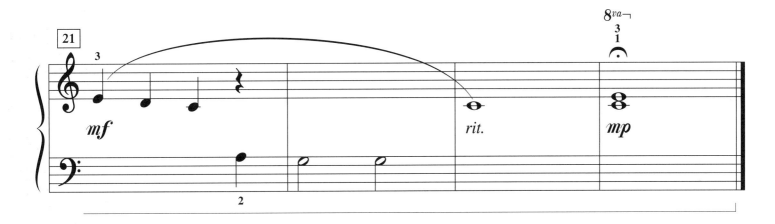

* Jump up 2 octaves.

Gus, the Groundhog

Groundhogs can move 700 pounds of soil to create long burrows with multiple chambers.
They have four toes on their front feet and five on their back feet.

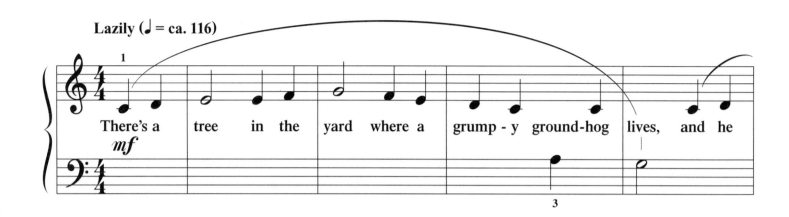

There's a tree in the yard where a grump-y ground-hog lives, and he

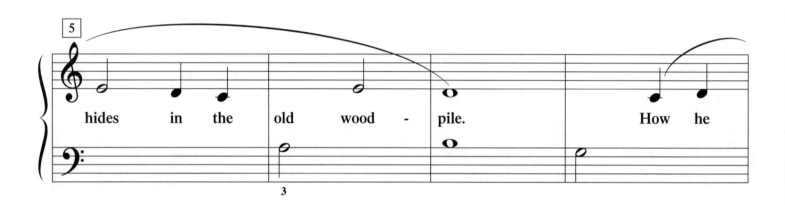

hides in the old wood - pile. How he

Teacher Duet: (Student plays 1 octave higher)

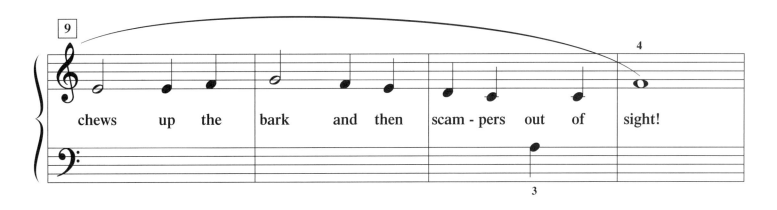

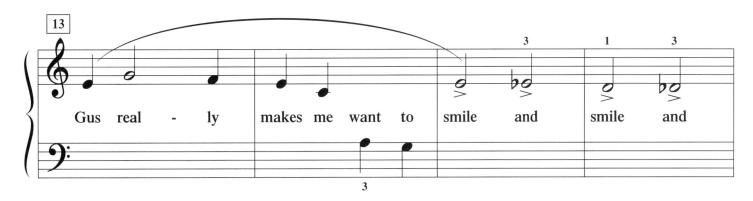

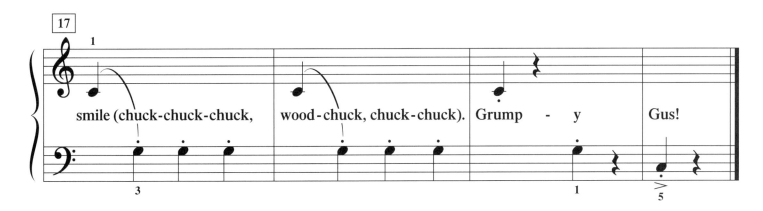

Travis the Trout

Fish have a very good sense of smell. They can not only smell a tasty night crawler a few yards away, but also smell bug spray transferred from your fingers to the fishing line.

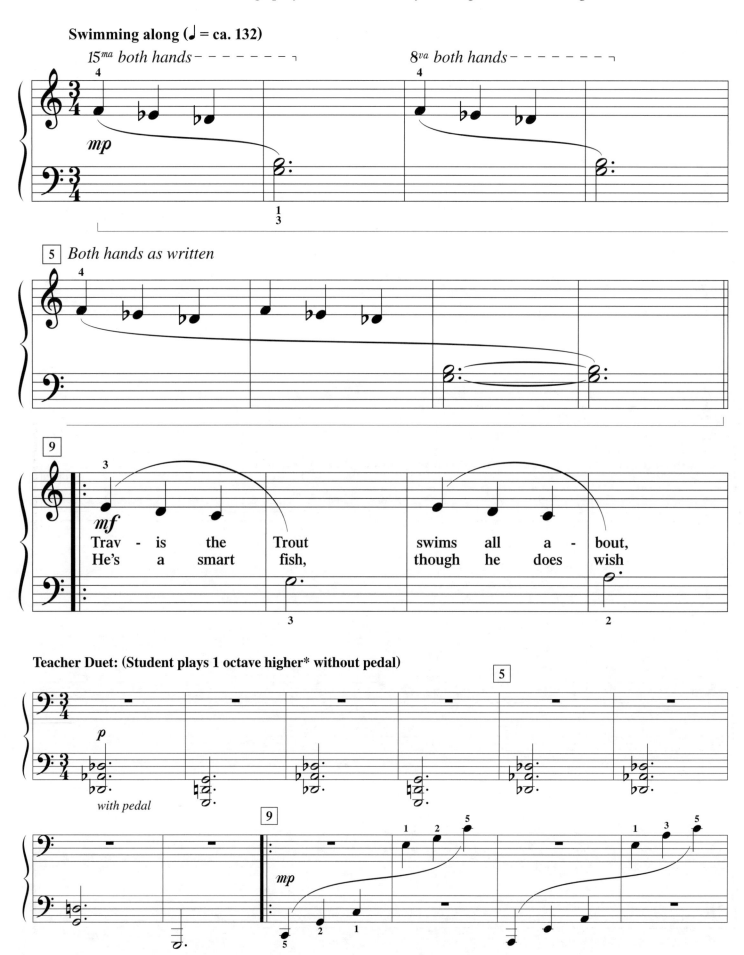

Teacher Duet: (Student plays 1 octave higher* without pedal)

* When played as a duet, student part actually begins 3 octaves higher than written (2 octaves + 1 octave for duet).

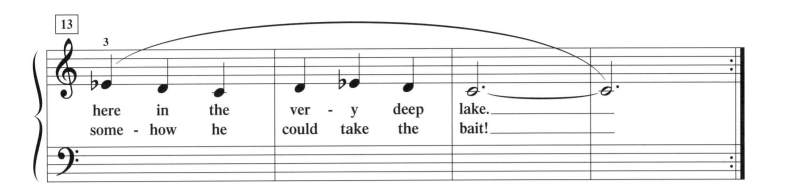

here   in   the   ver - y   deep   lake.

some - how   he   could   take   the   bait!

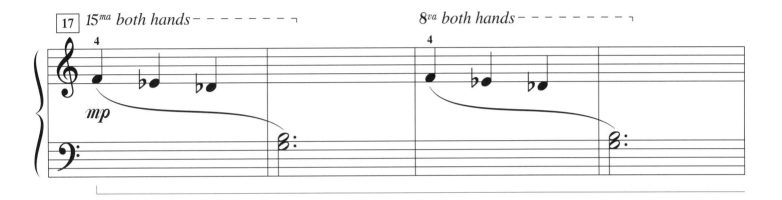

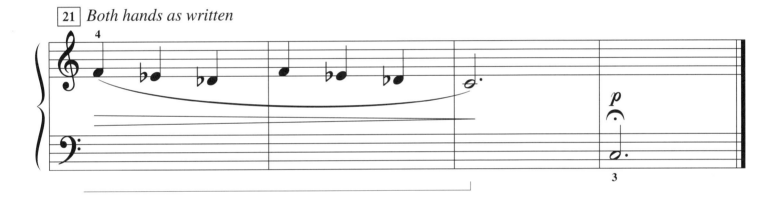

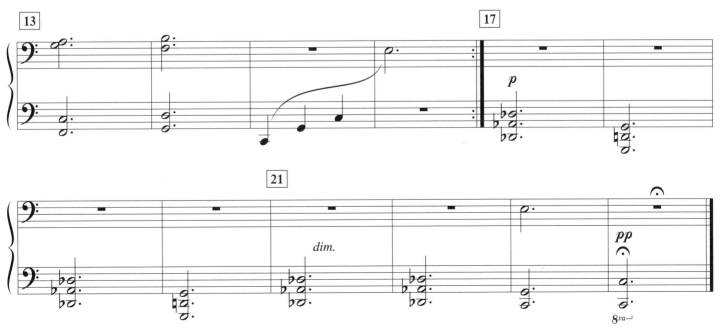

FJH1640

Chippie, the Chipmunk

You probably know that chipmunks have huge cheek pouches to gather food.
If you had cheek pouches as stretchy as a chipmunk's, you could fit eight oranges in your mouth!

Happily (♩ = ca. 144)

Lyrics:
There's a lit - tle chip - munk, Chip - pie is his name;
Leap - ing from the trees is his fun game.

Teacher Duet: (Student plays 1 octave higher*)

* When played as a duet, student part actually begins 3 octaves higher than written (2 octaves + 1 octave for duet).

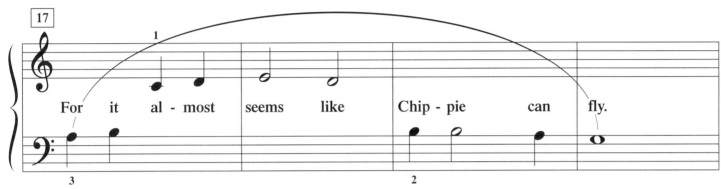

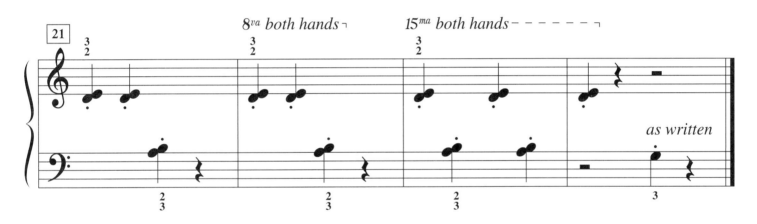

FJH1640

Lucy, the Lovely Loon

The loon is the state bird of Minnesota. Most bird bones are hollow and light;
loons have solid bones, and this extra weight helps them dive underwater in search of food.
They can also fly more than 75 miles per hour.

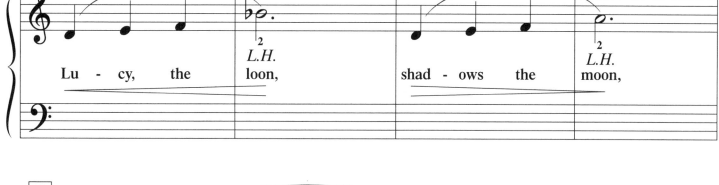

Lu - cy, the loon, shad - ows the moon,

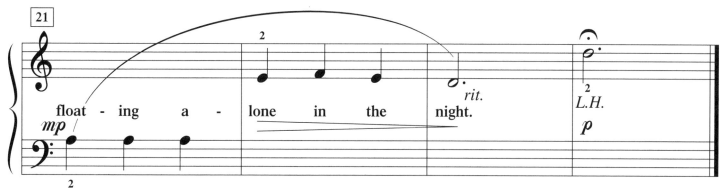

float - ing a - lone in the night.

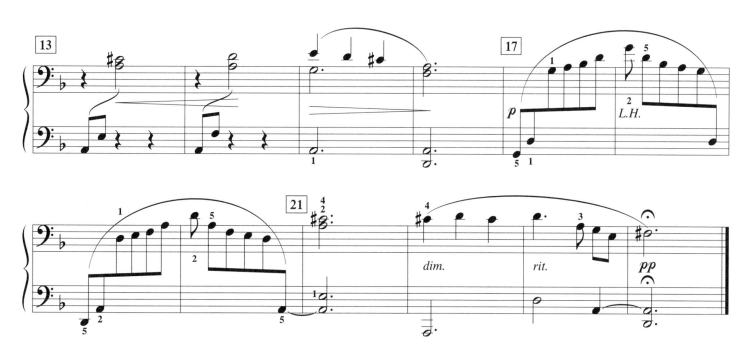

Ant March

Ants use their antennae not only for touch, but also for smell.
Did you know that they can lift twenty times their own body weight? Wow!

Steady and quick! (♩ = 132-138)

Teacher Duet: (Student plays 1 octave higher)

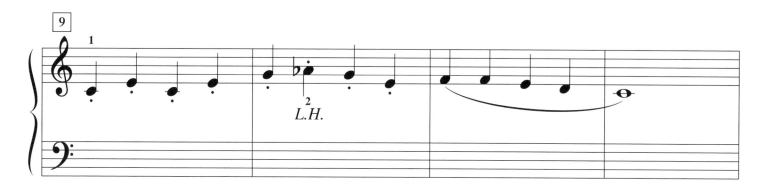

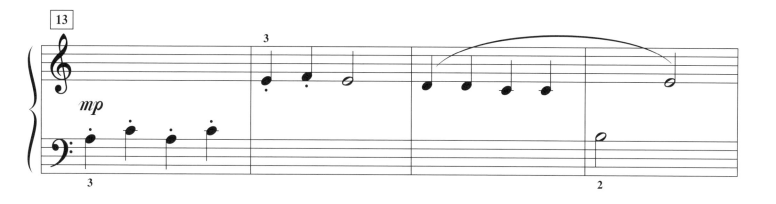

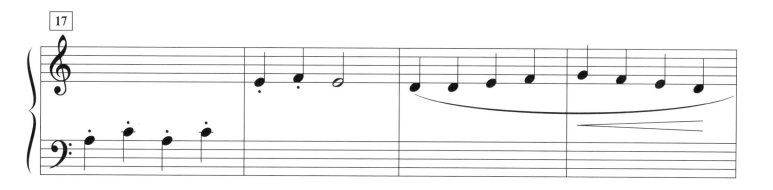

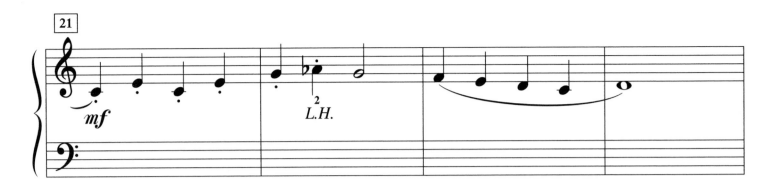

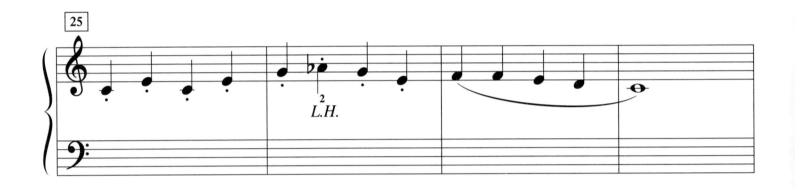

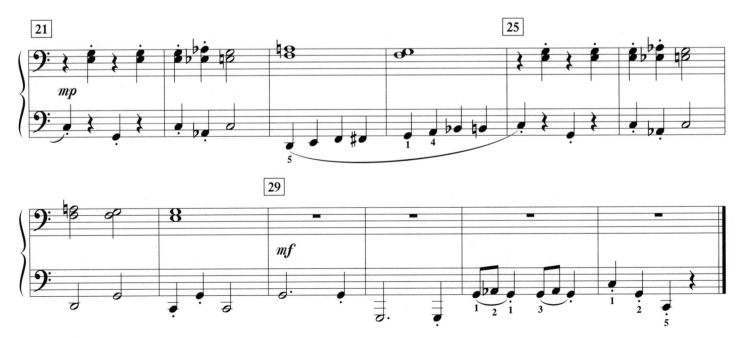